# COGAT Practice Questions

# for Grade 3 and 4

## 150 questions

### Verbal analogies, Verbal Classifications, and Sentence Completions

Publisher: CLP - Confident Learning Program

# Forward

The book you are about to read is designed to prepare students for the verbal batteries of the Cognitive Abilities Test (COGAT). The COGAT is a standardized test that measures a student's cognitive abilities, including their ability to understand and use language. The questions in this book are specifically tailored to test students' proficiency at the third and fourth-grade levels.

The questions in this book are challenging and aim to test students' understanding of abstract concepts and their ability to use advanced vocabulary in context. The multiple-choice format of the questions allows students to have several possibilities to choose from, making the test fair and challenging simultaneously.

This book will not only help students to improve their performance on the COGAT, but also to develop their overall language skills. It is an excellent resource for students, teachers, and parents who want to help their children excel in language and cognitive abilities.

Additionally, the book covers all the verbal batteries of the COGAT, including verbal classification, verbal reasoning, and sentence completion, with practice questions and explanations for each. With this book as a guide, students will be well-prepared to tackle the COGAT and demonstrate their mastery of language and cognitive abilities.

# Table of Content

Forward..................................................................................ii

Questions: Verbal Analogies ......................................................1

Questions: Verbal Classification.................................................18

Questions: Sentence Completion ...............................................35

Answers: Verbal Analogies .......................................................52

Answers: Verbal Classification...................................................58

Answers: Sentence Completion .................................................63

# Questions: Verbal Analogies

1. If "hat" is related to "coat", then "gloves" are related to which of the following?

    A) Scarf

    B) Sunglasses

    C) Belt

    D) Watch

    E) Boots

2. If "book" is related to "library", then "car" is related to which of the following

    A) Field

    B) Dealership

    C) Racing

    D) Wheels

    E) Driving

3. If "sofa" is related to "carpet", then "curtain" is related to which of the following?

    A) Lamp

    B) Picture frame

    C) Vase

    D) Window

    E) Table

4. If "egg" is related to "frying pan", then "pasta" is related to which of the following?

    A) Soup bowl

    B) Rice cooker

    C) Steamer

    D) Stock pot

    E) Pressure cooker

5. If "clock" is related to "alarm", then "watch" is related to which of the following?

    A) Timer

    B) Calendar

    C) Calculator

    D) Compass

    E) Stopwatch

6. If "Screwdriver" is related to "Screw", then "Hammer" is related to which of the following?

    A) Saw

    B) Nail

    C) Paintbrush

    D) Drill

    E) Wrench

7. If "Wheel" is related to "Car", then "Propeller" is related to which of the following?

      A) Motorcycle

      B) Skateboard

      C) Train

      D) Bicycle

      E) Boat

8. If "proud" is related to "arrogant", then "humble" is related to which of the following?

      A. Modest

      B. Shy

      C. Timid

      D. Bold

      E. Happy

9. If "Needle" is related to "Thread", then "Pencil" is related to which of the following?

      A) Paper

      B) Eraser

      C) Scissors

      D) Ruler

      E) Marker

10. If "Raincoat" is related to "Rain", then "Umbrella" is related to which of the following?

        A) Snow

        B) Sun

        C) Wind

        D) Fire

        E) Thunder

11. If "Candle" is related to "Wick", then "Lighter" is related to which of the following?

        A) Matches

        B) Firewood

        C) Charcoal

        D) Gas stove

        E) Kerosene

12. If "Garden hose" is related to "Water", then "Lawn mower" is related to which of the following?

        A) Fertilizer

        B) Tree

        C) Flower

        D) Hedge

        E) Grass

13. If "Canada" is related to "America", then "Russia" is related to which of the following?

        A) England

        B) Australia

        C) India

        D) China

        E) Saudi Arab

14. If "Potato" is related to "Fryer", then "Onion" is related to which of the following?

        A) Grater

        B) Juicer

        C) Blender

        D) Can opener

        E) Toaster

15. If "Thermometer" is related to "Temperature", then "Barometer" is related to which of the following?

        A) Altitude

        B) Pressure

        C) Humidity

        D) Wind

        E) Rain

16. If "Shampoo" is related to "Hair", then "Soap" is related to which of the following?

        A) Laundry

        B) Piping

        C) Cleaning

        D) Shaving

        E) Cooking

17. If "Battery" is related to "Electricity", then "Fuel" is related to which of the following?

        A) Solar Energy

        B) Wind Energy

        C) Hydro Energy

        D) Car Engine

        E) Nuclear Energy

18. If "Sausage" is related to "Grill", then "Steak" is related to which of the following?

        A) Blender

        B) Microwave

        C) Toaster

        D) Dishwasher

        E) Oven

19. If "Watering can" is related to "Plants", then "Hoe" is related to which of the following?

        A) Garden

        B) Farm

        C) Orchard

        D) Forest

        E) Desert

20. If "Glasses" are related to "Eyes", then "Hearing aids" are related to which of the following?

        A) Mouth

        B) Ears

        C) Nose

        D) Throat

        E) Brain

21. If "teacher" is related to "classroom", then "chef" is related to which of the following?

        A) Factory

        B) Store

        C) Office

        D) Kitchen

        E) Field

22. If "Book" is related to "Reading", then "Puzzle" is related to which of the following?

      A) Writing

      B) Thinking

      C) Watching

      D) Playing

      E) Listening

23. If "Kettle" is related to "Boiling water", then "Microwave" is related to which of the following?

      A) Cooling

      B) Heating

      C) Oiling

      D) Baking

      E) Frying

24. If "Oil painting" is related to "Canvas", then "Sculpture" is related to which of the following?

      A) Chocolate

      B) Device

      C) Marble

      D) Fabric

      E) Dishes

25. If "Ladder" is related to "Height", then "Wheelbarrow" is related to which of the following?

    A) Weight

    B) Length

    C) Width

    D) Volume

    E) Area

26. If "telescope" is related to "stars", then "microscope" is related to which of the following?

    A) Planets

    B) Cells

    C) Landscapes

    D) Animals

    E) Buildings

27. If "Clock" is related to "Time", then "Calculator" is related to which of the following?

    A) Language

    B) Science

    C) Math

    D) History

    E) Geography

28. If "Guitar" is related to "Musical Instrument", then "Microphone" is related to which of the following?

        A) Sound

        B) Light

        C) Color

        D) Temperature

        E) Pressure

29. If "violin" is related to "strings", then "piano" is related to which of the following?

        A) Guitar

        B) Drums

        C) Keys

        D) Horns

        E) Harmonica

30. If "Soccer" is related to "kick", then "baseball" is related to which of the following?

        A) Pass

        B) Jump

        C) Swing

        D) Rotate

        E) Swim

31. If "Wheelbarrow" is related to "Gardening", then "Shovel" is related to which of the following?

       A) Cleaning

       B) Painting

       C) Salting

       D) Construction

       E) Woodworking

32. If "Kettle" is related to "Boiling water", then "Blender" is related to which of the following?

       A) Mixing

       B) Stirring

       C) Heating

       D) Cooling

       E) Baking

33. If "Ladder" is related to "Height", then "Ruler" is related to which of the following?

       A) Cleaning

       B) Construction

       C) Decoration

       D) Cooking

       E) Measurement

34. If "Strawberry" are related to "Mango", then "Lettuce" is related to which of the following?

        A) Chicken

        B) Egg

        C) Cheese

        D) Apples

        E) Zucchini

35. If "Seeds" is related to "Gardening", then "Yarn" is related to which of the following?

        A) Knitting

        B) Sewing

        C) Weaving

        D) Crochet

        E) Beading

36. If "Thermos" is related to "Hot beverage", then "Cooler" is related to which of the following?

        A) Hot meal

        B) Cold beverage

        C) Ice

        D) Frozen food

        E) Fish

37. If "Skateboard" is related to "Skatepark", then "Bicycle" is related to which of the following?

    A) Greenfield

    B) Roller rink

    C) Bike trail

    D) Running track

    E) Swimming pool

38. If "Calculator" is related to "Math", then "Dictionary" is related to which of the following?

    A) Language

    B) Science

    C) History

    D) Geography

    E) Religion

39. If "Suitcase" is related to "Travel", then "Briefcase" is related to which of the following?

    A) School

    B) Work

    C) Shopping

    D) Leisure

    E) Sport

40. If "Laptop" is related to "Internet", then "Television" is related to which of the following?

      A) Computing

      B) Blogging

      C) Gaming

      D) Broadcasting

      E) Video conferencing

41. If "Cookbook" is related to "Recipes", then "Map" is related to which of the following?

      A) Navigation

      B) Photography

      C) Writing

      D) Music

      E) Painting

42. If "Flashlight" is related to "Dark", then "Sunscreen" is related to which of the following?

      A) Wind

      B) Cold

      C) Heat

      D) Sun

      E) Rain

43. If "Mouse" is related to "Cat", then "Deer" is related to which of the following?

        A) Sloth

        B) Monkey

        C) Elephant

        D) Ant

        E) Tiger

44. If "Hammer" is related to "Nail", then "Wrench" is related to which of the following?

        A) Pipe

        B) Bolt

        C) Nut

        D) Drill

        E) Saw

45. If "ocean" is related to "waves", then "desert" is related to which of the following?

        A) Dunes

        B) Forests

        C) Mountains

        D) Rivers

        E) Snow

46. If "Certificate" is related to "Training", then "Medal / Prize" is related to which of the following?

    A) News

    B) Weather

    C) Tournament

    D) Biking

    E) Parties


47. If "dog" is related to "bark", then "cat" is related to which of the following?

    A) Hoot

    B) Growl

    C) Whistle

    D) Howl

    E) Purr


48. If "book" is related to "author", then "movie" is related to which of the following?

    A) Actor

    B) Writer

    C) Composer

    D) Director

    E) Critic

49. If "apple" is related to "fruit", then "carrot" is related to which of the following?

       A) Fish

       B) Meat

       C) Dairy

       D) Vegetable

       E) Grain

50. If "laptop" is related to "device", then "car" is related to which of the following?

       A) Furniture

       B) Equipment

       C) Biking

       D) train

       E) vehicle

# Questions: Verbal Classification

51. Choose the word that best fits with the group.

Couch Sofa Recliner

        A) Armchair

        B) Electronics

        C) Sheet

        D) Television

        E) Appliances

52. Choose the word that best fits with the group.

Saw Drill Screwdriver

        A) Hardware

        B) Appliances

        C) Wrench

        D) Tools

        E) Gardening

53. Choose the word that best fits with the group.

Baseball Football Soccer

        A) Sports

        B) Hobbies

        C) Volleyball

        D) Exercises

        E) Team activities

54. Choose the word that best fits with the group.

Book Magazine Newspaper

A) Food

B) Paper

C) Office supplies

D) E-book

E) Postcard


55. Choose the word that best fits with the group.

Blender Juicer Food processor

A) Stone

B) Home appliances

C) Spray Gun

D) Cutting board

E) Mixer


56. Choose the word that best fits with the group.

Piano Guitar Violin

A) Harp

B) Trampoline

C) Spoon

D) Phone

E) Shoe

57. Choose the word that best fits with the group.

Shampoo Soap Lotion

        A) Detergent

        B) Conditioner

        C) Brush

        D) Hose

        E) Soybean

58. Choose the word that best fits with the group.

Gas Electric Hybrid

        A) Trains

        B) Bicycles

        C) Boats

        D) Solar

        E) Cars

59. Choose the word that best fits with the group.

Apple Banana Orange

        A) Meat

        B) Tomato

        C) Cake

        D) Fruits

        E) Pineapple

60. Choose the word that best fits with the group.

Beach Mountain Desert

        A) Statue

        B) Building

        C) Forest

        D) School

        E) Stadium


61. Choose the word that best fits with the group.

Ruler Compass Protractor

        A) Bowl

        B) Knife

        C) Pencil

        D) Duct tape

        E) Can


62. Choose the word that best fits with the group.

Water Milk Juice

        A) Cookie

        B) Food

        C) Soda

        D) Tylenol

        E) Pasta

63. Choose the word that best fits with the group.

Jacket Scarf Gloves

        A) Hiking Stick

        B) Sunglass

        C) Ring

        D) Mittens

        E) Outdoor gear

64. Choose the word that best fits with the group.

Laptop Tablet Smartphone

        A) Radio

        B) Playing cards

        C) Kaleidoscope

        D) Desktop Computer

        E) Saw

65. Choose the word that best fits with the group.

Coffee Tea Hot chocolate

        A) Juice

        B) Pepsi

        C) Cake

        D) Mousse

        E) Cappuccino

66. Choose the word that best fits with the group.

Hiking boots Sneakers Flip-flops

        A) Outerwear

        B) Headwear

        C) Footwear

        D) Sandals

        E) Accessories

67. Choose the word that best fits with the group.

Shower Bathtub Sink

        A) Home decor

        B) Laundry

        C) Toilet

        D) Garden Hose

        E) Bathroom fixtures

68. Choose the word that best fits with the group.

Bagel Croissant Donut

        A) Soup

        B) Egg

        C) Cheese

        D) Muffin

        E) Pizza

69. Choose the word that best fits with the group.

Hotel Motel Inn

        A) Mall

        B) Restaurants

        C) Park

        D) Hostel

        E) Entertainment venues


70. Choose the word that best fits with the group.

Tomato Cucumber Lettuce

        A) Fruits

        B) Vegetables

        C) Spices

        D) Meats

        E) Carrot


71. Choose the word that best fits with the group.

Email Chat Video call

        A) Voice call

        B) YouTube

        C) Social Media

        D) Nintendo

        E) Productivity tools

72. Choose the word that best fits with the group.

Frog Kangaroo Grasshopper

> A) Springbok
>
> B) Crab
>
> C) Turtle
>
> D) Squid
>
> E) Sloth

73. Choose the word that best fits with the group.

Pen Pencil Marker

> A) Writing instruments
>
> B) Desk
>
> C) Measuring tools
>
> D) Office equipment
>
> E) Paper

74. Choose the word that best fits with the group.

Beef Mutton Chicken

> A) Lamb
>
> B) Fish
>
> C) Meat
>
> D) Grains
>
> E) Dairy

75. Choose the word that best fits with the group.

African lion Giraffe Rhino

A) Otter

B) American Bison

C) Deer

D) Mountain Gorilla

E) Penguin


76. Choose the word that best fits with the group.

Ketchup Mustard Mayo

A) Mozzarella

B) Pepper

C) Butter

D) Peanut

E) Ranch


77. Choose the word that best fits with the group.

Wheel Spindle Merry-go-round

A) Bus

B) Fan

C) Handle

D) Creeb

E) Table

78. Choose the word that best fits with the group.

Coach Doctor Nurse

        A) Medicine

        B) Syringe

        C) Engineering

        D) Plumber

        E) Hospital

79. Choose the word that best fits with the group.

Kite Hawk Falcon

        A) Albatross

        B) Ostrich

        C) Emu

        D) Penguin

        E) Hunter

80. Choose the word that best fits with the group.

Honda Toyota Ford

        A) Home Depot

        B) Lincoln

        C) Disney

        D) GAP

        E) CCM

81. Choose the word that best fits with the group.

Mascara Lipstick Nail polish

        A) Eyeliner

        B) Makeup

        C) Shampoo

        D) Fragrances

        E) Soap


82. Choose the word that best fits with the group.

Dog, Cat, Snake

        A) Rabbit

        B) Hyena

        C) Elephant

        D) Deer

        E) Goat


Choose the word that best fits with the group.

83. Chess Checkers Tic-tac-toe

        A) Baseball

        B) Card games

        C) Board games

        D) Video games

        E) Cribbage

84. Choose the word that best fits with the group.

Pizza Burger Tacos

        A) Fast food

        B) Seafood

        C) Burrito

        D) Mexican food

        E) Stew


85. Choose the word that best fits with the group.

Asia Europe Africa

        A) Canada

        B) Australia

        C) Russia

        D) Oceania

        E) Brazil


86. Choose the word that best fits with the group.

Rock Boulder Tree

        A) Statue

        B) Moon

        C) Ball

        D) Building

        E) Kettle

87. Choose the word that best fits with the group.

Blanket, Throw, Quilt

        A) Duvet

        B) Chair

        C) Motor

        D) Stick

        E) Scratcher

88. Choose the word that best fits with the group.

College School University

        A) Campus

        B) Stadium

        C) Road

        D) Terminal

        E) Television

89. Choose the word that best fits with the group.

Skirt Dress Blouse

        A) Blanket

        B) Shorts

        C) Footwear

        D) Shoe

        E) Fork

90. Choose the word that best fits with the group.

Shark Dolphin Whale

       A) Sparrow

       B) Birds

       C) Flying fish

       D) Tortoise

       E) Penguin


91. Choose the word that best fits with the group.

Bicycle Skateboard Roller skates

       A) Soccer

       B) Golf

       C) Wheel

       D) Scooter

       E) Pen


92. Choose the word that best fits with the group.

Salad Soup Stew

       A) Chowder

       B) Hot meals

       C) Desserts

       D) Snacks

       E) Sprite

93. Choose the word that best fits with the group.

Roses Daisies Tulips

A) Trees

B) Flowers

C) Fruits

D) Lily

E) Squash

94. Choose the word that best fits with the group.

Guitar Piano Drums

A) Water gun

B) Skipping

C) Power tools

D) Flute

E) Trampoline

95. Choose the word that best fits with the group.

Gold Silver Bronze

A) Metals

B) Plastics

C) Stones

D) Platinum

E) Fabric

96. Choose the word that best fits with the group.

Spatula Ladle Whisk

        A) Can

        B) Spoon

        C) Measuring tools

        D) Sink

        E) Drill bit


97. Choose the word that best fits with the group.

Bear Wolf Moose

        A) Chicken

        B) Cow

        C) Caribou

        D) Salmon

        E) Reptiles


98. Choose the word that best fits with the group.

Nurse Doctor Surgeon

        A) Teachers

        B) Lawyers

        C) Engineers

        D) Dentists

        E) Chefs

99. Choose the word that best fits with the group.

Leonardo da Vinci, Van Gough, Michelangelo

        A) Pablo Picasso

        B) Einstein

        C) Abraham Lincoln

        D) Nikola Tesla

        E) Isaac Newton


100.      Choose the word that best fits with the group.

Snow Hail Rain

        A) Thunder

        B) Wind Gust

        C) Drought

        D) Fire

        E) Sleet

# Questions: Sentence Completion

101.     I think it's just a couple _____ that we wish we could take back.

    A) fun

    B) game

    C) memories

    D) mistakes

    E) food


102.     John put the blanket back on the dryer as it was still _____.

    A) wrinkled

    B) smooth

    C) wet

    D) fluffy

    E) heavy

103.     David put the painting back on the easel as it was still _____.

    A) unfinished

    B) complete

    C) abstract

    D) realistic

    E) colorful

104.    The _____ of the sun sets in the west.

    A. direction

    B. color

    C. shape

    D. size

    E. Sky

105.    The _____ of a person's character can be determined by their actions.

    A. integrity

    B. reputation

    C. kindness

    D. intelligence

    E. Politeness

106.    The _____ of the book is the author's main idea or message.

    A. theme

    B. plot

    C. setting

    D. protagonist

    E. text

107.     Alex put the guitar back in its case as it was still _____.

      A) out of tune

      B) in tune

      C) broken

      D) new

      E) dirty

108.     Dogs are _____ pets that love to play and bark.

      A) Grumpy

      B) Loyal

      C) Aloof

      D) Hostile

      E) Independent

109.     The _____ of the tree is important for its growth.

      A. root

      B. trunk

      C. bark

      D. leaf

      E. meat

110.    The _____ of the city was bustling with activity.

A. downtown

B. countryside

C. seashore

D. suburb

E. village


111.    The _____ of the experiment was to test the reaction of the plant to different light levels.

A. purpose

B. hypothesis

C. procedure

D. result

E. picture


112.    The _____ of the concert was incredible, with the musicians playing to perfection.

A. performance

B. sound

C. lighting

D. crowd

E. colour

113.    The _____ of the school is to provide quality education to all students.

A. mission

B. teachers

C. goal

D. objective

E. value


114.    The _____ of the story is where the events take place.

A. setting

B. genre

C. conflict

D. characterization

E. purpose


115.    The _____ of the basketball game was intense, with both teams fighting for the lead.

A. competition

B. match

C. game

D. tournament

E. tv

116.     The _____ of the volcano is the point where the magma or lava comes out.

   A. crater

   B. eruption

   C. magma

   D. ash

   E. hole

117.     The _____ of the plant is the process of using energy from the sun to make food.

   A. photosynthesis

   B. pollination

   C. germination

   D. fertilization

   E. agriculture

118.     The _____ of the poem is the author's attitude or feeling towards the subject.

   A. tone

   B. rhyme

   C. meter

   D. stanza

   E. text

119.     The _____ of the city is the people who live in it.

A. population

B. culture

C. architecture

D. economy

E. color


120.     The _____ of the mountain is the highest point on it.

A. summit

B. peak

C. ridge

D. valley

E. path


121.     The _____ of the government is to serve and protect the citizens.

A. purpose

B. function

C. duty

D. goal

E. play

122.　　The _____ of the essay is the main argument or point the author is trying to make.

A. thesis

B. conclusion

C. introduction

D. evidence

E. poem

123.　　The _____ of the game is to get the ball into the opponent's goal.

A. objective

B. rule

C. strategy

D. team

E. crowd

124.　　Even though it was raining, the little girl was _____ to go outside.

A. reluctant to

B. determined

C. playing

D. soak

E. sleep

125.     The _____ of the river is the direction in which it flows.

    A. course

    B. width

    C. depth

    D. speed

    E. water


126.     The _____ of the play is the order of events and how they unfold.

    A. structure

    B. theme

    C. dialogue

    D. setting

    E. dial


127.     The _____ of the music is the combination of sounds and rhythms.

    A. composition

    B. melody

    C. harmony

    D. rhythm

    E. tune

128.     The _____ of the painting is the way the artist uses colors, lines, and shapes.

   A. style

   B. subject

   C. medium

   D. technique

   E. time


129.     The _____ of the research is to gather information and data on a specific topic.

   A. objective

   B. methodology

   C. conclusion

   D. hypothesis

   E. process


130.     The _____ of the company is the group of people who own and manage it.

   A. management

   B. employees

   C. shareholders

   D. customers

   E. worker

131.　　The _____ of the ecosystem is the balance of living and nonliving things in it.

A. equilibrium

B. diversity

C. adaptation

D. reproduction

E. capacity


132.　　The _____ of the math problem is the unknown or missing value that needs to be found.

A. unknown

B. solution

C. equation

D. variable

E. problem


133.　　The _____ of the debate is the main point of disagreement or contention.

A. topic

B. argument

C. talk

D. evidence

E. time

134.     The _____ of the poem is the pattern of stressed and unstressed syllables in the lines.

A. meter

B. rhyme

C. imagery

D. alliteration

E. fun

135.     The _____ of the comedy is to entertain the audience and make them laugh.

A. function

B. genre

C. setting

D. plot

E. coolness

136.     The _____ is a planet in our solar system known for its rings.

A. Saturn

B. Jupiter

C. Uranus

D. Mercury

137.    The _____ is a large mammal that lives in the ocean.

    A. shark

    B. lion

    C. elephant

    D. whale

    E. Turtle


138.    The _____ is a type of bird known for its long neck and legs.

    A. Ostrich

    B. Falcon

    C. Sparrow

    D. Blue Jay

    E. Eagle

139.    The _____ is a measure of how much matter is in an object.

    A. weight

    B. volume

    C. mass

    D. length

    D. Density.

140.     The _____ is a group of stars that form a recognizable pattern.

        A. galaxy

        B. constellation

        C. meteor

        D. comet

        E. Asteroid

141.     The _____ is a type of simple machine that consists of a rope, cable or chain wrapped around a grooved wheel.

        A. lever

        B. inclined plane

        C. screw

        D. pulley

        E. Gear

142.     The sky is blue because of the way the _____ scatters sunlight.

        A. Moon's atmosphere

        B. Earth's atmosphere

        C. Sun's atmosphere

        D. Heat

        E. Magnetic Wave

143.     The _____ is a type of ecosystem that is typically found in very cold regions.

    A. desert

    B. rainforest

    C. tundra

    D. coral reef

    E. savanna

144.     The _____ is a type of plant that has small leaves and reproduces through spores.

    A. cactus

    B. rose

    C. fern

    D. sunflower

    E. Mango

145.     The little boy _____ his ice cream cone.

    a. Licked

    b. Bit

    c. Smashed

    d. Ate

    e. Dropped

146.    The dog _____ his tail when he saw his owner.

    A. Wagged

    B. Bites

    C. Licked

    D. Jumped

    E. Cried


147.    I like to _____ my bike around the neighborhood.

    A. Ride

    B. Walk

    C. Drive

    D. Fly

    E. Roll


148.    Suddenly a large old _____ drove up, and an old lady sat in it

    A. chair

    B. Ideas

    C. carriage

    D. swing

    E. boat

149.    I went up to the _____ where I met a polar
    bear

    A. Africa

    B. Arctic

    C. Antartca

    D. Australia

    E. Amazon


150.    An island is surrounded by _____.

    A. Sand

    B. Forrest

    C. Water

    D. Buidling

    E. Rock

# Answers: Verbal Analogies

**1 A**

Explanation: "Gloves" are often worn in cold weather along with a coat and a hat, so they are related to the item "Scarf" which is also commonly worn in cold weather to keep the neck warm.

**2 A**

ExplanatiBn: As bookes are stored in the library, cars are stored in dealership for sale.

**3 D**

Explanation: "Curtain" is used to cover the window and control the light coming into a room; it is related to "window" as it needs to be installed on it.

**4 D**

Explanation: "Pasta" is often cooked in a "Stock pot" which is a large pot used for boiling pasta, soups, and other foods that require a lot of water.

**5 A**

Explanation: "Watch" is a device used to tell time and is often equipped with a "Timer" which allows the user to measure elapsed time.

**6 B**

Explanation: A "Hammer" is used to drive "Nails" into wood or other materials and is therefore related to "Nail".

**7 E**

Explanation: The propeller is a device that creates thrust for boats and ships and related to "Boat".

**8 A**

Explanation: Modest refers to being unassuming and not having excessive pride, which is similar to "humble".

**9 A**

Explanation: Pencil is used to write and draw on paper, it is therefore related to "Paper".

**10 B**

Explanation: Umbrella are mostly used to protect oneself from the sun, therefore it is related to "Sun".

**11 A**

Explanation: A lighter is a small device that creates a flame, and it is commonly used to light matches and candles, it is therefore related to "Matches".

**12 E**

Explanation: A lawn mower is an outdoor power tool used to mow grass, therefore related to "Grass".

**13 D**

Explanation: Canada and America are neighbours. So are Russia and China.

**14 A**

Explanation: Grater is a kitchen tool that is used to shred onions and other vegetables; it is therefore related to "Onion".

**15 B**

Explanation: Barometer is a device that measures atmospheric pressure; it is, therefore, related to "Pressure".

**16 A**

Explanation: Soap is a cleaning agent; it is therefore related to "Laundry".

**17 D**

Explanation: Fuel is used to power engines; it is therefore related to "Car".

**18 E**

Explanation: Steak is usually cooked in an oven or on a grill, it is therefore related to "Oven".

19 A

Explanation: Hoe is a gardening tool used to till soil, it is therefore related to "Garden"

20 B

Explanation: Hearing aids are devices that help to amplify sound for people with hearing difficulties, and therefore it is related to "Ears".

21 D

Explanation: The correct answer is "kitchen" as it's where chefs cook and prepare food.

22 B

Explanation: Puzzles are mental challenges designed to keep you thinking, it is therefore related to "Thinking"

23 B

Explanation: Microwave is used for heating and cooking food, it is therefore related to "Heating"

24 C

Explanation: Sculptures are often made of materials like marble, metal, and wood, it is therefore related to "Marble"

25 A

Explanation: Wheelbarrow is used to move heavy loads, it is therefore related to "Weight"

26 B

Explanation: The correct answer is "cells" as microscope is used to observe small things like cells.

27 C

Explanation: Calculator is a device used for mathematical calculations, it is therefore related to "Math".

28 A

Explanation: Microphone is used to amplify or record sound, it is therefore related to "Sound"

29 C

Explanation: The correct answer is "keys" as they are the element of piano that produce the sound.

30 C

Explanation: Baseball bats are swung.

31 C

Explanation: A Shovel is a tool used to dig and move soil and other materials, it is therefore related to "Construction"

32 A

Explanation: A blender is a kitchen appliance used to blend or puree food, it is therefore related to "Mixing"

33 E

Explanation: A ruler is a tool used for measuring length and width, it is therefore related to "Measurement"

34 E

Explanation: Lettuce and Zucchini are vegetables.

35 A

Explanation: Yarn is a material often used for knitting, crocheting and weaving, it is therefore related to "Knitting"

36 B

Explanation: Cooler is a container used to keep things cold such as drinks or food, it is therefore related to "Cold beverage"

37 C

Explanation: A bicycle is often ridden on bike trails and roads, it is therefore related to "Bike trail".

38 A

Explanation: A dictionary is a reference book used for finding the meanings of words and checking spellings, it is related to "Language".

39 B

Explanation: A briefcase is a type of bag that is used to carry documents and other items for work, it is therefore related to "Work".

40 D

Explanation: Television is a device that is used to watch broadcasted shows and programming, it is therefore related to "Broadcasting".

41 A

Explanation: Navigation" is the correct answer because a map is used for finding directions and navigating to a desired location.

42 D

Explanation: Sunscreen is related to the sun because sunscreen is used to protect the skin from the harmful UV rays emitted by the sun, which can cause sunburn and skin cancer.

43 E

Explanation: Mice are hunted by Cats. And Deers are hunted by Tigers.

44 C

Explanation: Wrench is related to a nut because a wrench is a tool commonly used for tightening or loosening nuts and bolts.

45 A

Explanation: Dunes are found in deserts.

46 C

Explanation: A certificate is given after successful training. Medals / Prizes are given in tournaments after the wins.

47 E

Explanation: The expression of sounds of dogs are cats are bark and purrs, respectively.

48 D

Explanation: 'Book' is written by 'Authors,' and 'Movies' are directed by 'Directors'.

49 D

Explanation: 'Carrot' is a vegetable.

50 B

Explanation: 'Laptops' fall in the 'Device' group, whereas 'Cars' fall in the 'Vehicle' group.

# Answers: Verbal Classification

**51. A**

Explanation: Couch, Sofa, Recliner, and Armchair are all furniture.

**52. C**

Explanation: Saw, Drill, Screwdriver, and Wrench are all hardware tools.

**53. C**

Explanation: Baseball, Football, Soccer, and Volleyball are all outdoor games.

**54. D**

Explanation: Book, Magazine, Newspaper, and E-book are all reading materials.

**55. E**

Explanation: Blender, Juicer, Food processor, and Mixer all kitchen appliances.

**56. A**

Explanation: Piano, Guitar, Violin, and Harp are all musical instruments.

**57. B**

Explanation: Shampoo, Soap, Lotion, and Conditioner are all personal care products.

**58. D**

Explanation: Gas, Electric, Hybrid, and Solar are all energy sources for vehicles.

**59. E**

Explanation: Apple, Banana, Orange, and Pineapple are all fruits.

60. C

Explanation: Beach, Mountain, Desert, and Forest are all natural places.

61. C

Explanation: Ruler, Compass, Protractor, and Pencil are all stationery items.

62. C

Explanation: Water, Milk, Juice, and Soda are all drinks.

63. D

Explanation: Jacket, Scarf, Gloves, and Mittens are all winter cloths.

64. D

Explanation: Laptop, Tablet, Smartphone, and Desktop Computer are mainly electronic devices.

65. E

Explanation: Coffee, Tea, Hot, chocolate, and Latte all are mostly hot drinks.

66. D

Explanation: Hiking boots, Sneakers, Flip-flops, and Sandals are all footwears.

67. C

Explanation: Shower, Bathtub, Sink, and Toilet are all bathroom fittings.

68. D

Explanation: Bagel, Croissant, Donut, are Muffins all baked products.

69. D

Explanation: Hotel, Motel, Inn, and Hostel are place to stay at night (mostly).

70. E

Explanation: Tomato, Cucumber, Lettuce, and Carrot are all vegetables.

71. A

Explanation: Email, Chat, Video call, and Voice call are all communication methods.

72. A

Explanation: Frog Kangaroo Grasshopper and Springbok are all known for jumping.

73. E

Explanation: Pen Pencil Marker, and paper are all writing instruments.

74. A

Explanation: Beef, Mutton, Chicken, and lamb are all types of meat.

75. C

Explanation: African Lion, Giraffe, Rhino, and Mountain Gorilla are mainly found in Africa.

76. E

Explanation: Ketchup Mustard Mayo, and Ranch are types of condiments.

77. B

Explanation: All of Wheel, Spindle, Merry-go-round, and fan rotate

78. D

Explanation: Coach, Doctor, Nurse, and Plumber are professions.

79. A

Explanation: Kite Hawk Falcon, and Albatross are high-flying birds.

80. B

Explanation: Honda Toyota Ford, and Lincoln are the car brand names.

81. A

Explanation: Mascara Lipstick Nail polish and Eyeliner are make-up items.

82. B

Explanation: Dog, Cat, Snake, and Hyenas are all hunters.

83. E

Explanation: Chess Checkers Tic-tac-toe, and Cribbage are all board games.

84. C

Explanation: Pizza, Burger, Tacos, and Burritos are all fast foods.

85. D

Explanation: Asia, Europe, Africa, and Oceania are all continents. The rests are countries.

86. B

Explanation: Rock, Boulder, Tree, and Moon are all natural items.

87. A

Explanation: Blanket, Throw, Quilt and Duvet are all mostly fabric items.

88. A

Explanation: College, School, University, and Campus are all related to education.

89. B

Explanation: Skirt, Dress, Blouse, and Shorts are dresses.

90. C

Explanation: Shark, Dolphin, Whale, and Flying fish are sea creatures.

91. D

Explanation: Bicycle, Skateboard, Roller skates, and Scooter are mode of transportation.

92.  A

Explanation: Salad, Soup, Stew, and Chowder are hot meals.

93.  D

Explanation: Roses, Daisies, Tulips, and Lily are flowers.

94.  D

Explanation: Guitar, Piano, Drums, and flute are musical instruments.

95.  D

Explanation: Gold, Silver, Bronze, and Platinum are metals.

96.  B

Explanation: Spatula, Ladle, Whisk, and Spoon are kitchen utensils.

97.  C

Explanation: Bear, Wolf, Moose, and Caribou are wild animals.

98.  D

Explanation: Nurse, Doctor, Surgeon, and Dentists are healthcare professionals.

99.  A

Explanation: Leonardo da Vinci, Van Gough, Michelangelo, and Pablo Picasso are artists.

100. E

Explanation: Snow, Hail, Rain and Sleet are all natural phenomena that has water.

# Answers: Sentence Completion

101. D) Mistakes

Explanation: People sometimes wish to take back the mistakes to so that they didn't fall into danger or bad situation.

102. C) wet

Explanation: John put the blanket back on the dryer as it was still wet, meaning it had not yet been dried and was still damp.

103. A) unfinished

Explanation: David put the painting back on the easel as it was still unfinished, meaning it had not yet been completed and still needed more work.

104. A. direction

Explanation: The direction of the sun sets in the west, meaning that the sun appears to move from east to west and sets in the west.

105. A. integrity

Explanation: The integrity of a person's character can be determined by their actions, meaning their actions reflect their moral principles and values.

106. A. theme

Explanation: The theme of the book is the author's main idea or message, meaning the underlying message or subject that the author wants to convey.

107. B) out of tune

Explanation: Alex put the guitar back in its case as it was still out of tune, meaning it was not ready to play.

108. B) Loyal

Explanation: Dogs are famous for their loyalty

109.A. root

Explanation: The root of the tree is important for its growth, as it absorbs water and nutrients from the soil and anchors the tree in place.

110.A. downtown

Explanation: The downtown of the city was bustling with activity, meaning the central business district was full of people and activity.

111.A. purpose

Explanation: The purpose of the experiment was to test the reaction of the plant to different light levels, meaning the aim of the experiment is to study how the plant responds to different levels of light.

112.A. performance

Explanation: The performance of the concert was incredible, meaning the musicians played to perfection and the overall musical performance was outstanding.

113.A. mission

Explanation: The mission of the school is to provide quality education to all students, meaning the school's purpose is to provide the best education possible for all students.

114.A. setting

Explanation: The setting of the story is where the events take place, meaning the physical location and time period in which the events of the story occur.

115.A. competition

Explanation: The competition of the basketball game was intense, meaning both teams were fighting for the lead and the game was competitive and challenging.

116.A. crater

Explanation: The crater of the volcano is the point where the magma or lava comes out, meaning the opening at the top of the volcano where the molten rock and ash are erupted.

117.A. photosynthesis

Explanation: The process of the plant is the process of using energy from the sun to make food, meaning the way plants convert light energy into chemical energy to produce food.

118.A. tone

Explanation: The tone of the poem is the author's attitude or feeling towards the subject, meaning the overall feeling or emotion conveyed in the poem.

119.A. population

Explanation: The population of the city is the people who live in it, meaning the number of people residing in the city.

120.A. summit

Explanation: The summit of the mountain is the highest point on it, meaning the highest point or peak of the mountain.

121.A. purpose

Explanation: The purpose of the government is to serve and protect the citizens, meaning the role of the government is to serve the best interests of the citizens and ensure their safety and well-being.

122.A. thesis

Explanation: The thesis of the essay is the main argument or point the author is trying to make, meaning the main idea or point the author is trying to prove or argue in the essay.

123.A. objective

Explanation: The objective of the game is to get the ball into the opponent's goal, meaning the aim of the game is to score points by getting the ball into the opposing team's goal.

124.A) determined

Explanations: Rain would make the girl drenched in water and might be inconvenient for her. But still wanted to go outside as a determined person.

125.A) course

Explanations: the course of a river refers to the direction in which it flows.

126.A) structure

Explanations: the structure of a play refers to the order of events and how they unfold.

127.A) composition

Explanations: the composition of music refers to the combination of sounds and rhythms.

128.A) style

Explanations: the style of a painting refers to the way the artist uses colors, lines, and shapes.

129.A) objective

Explanations: the objective of the research is to gather information and data on a specific topic.

130.A) management

Explanations: the management of a company refers to the group of people who own and manage it.

131.A) equilibrium

Explanations: the equilibrium of an ecosystem refers to the balance of living and nonliving things in it.

132.A) unknown

Explanations: the unknown of a math problem refers to the missing value that needs to be found.

133.A) topic

Explanations: the topic of a debate refers to the main point of disagreement or contention.

134.A) meter

Explanations: the meter of a poem refers to the pattern of stressed and unstressed syllables in the lines.

135.A) function

Explanations: the function of a comedy is to entertain the audience and make them laugh.

136.A) Saturn

Explanations: Saturn is a planet in our solar system known for its rings.

137.D) whale

Explanations: a whale is a large mammal that lives in the ocean.

138.A) Ostrich

Explanations: Ostrich is a type of bird known for its long neck and legs.

139.C) mass

Explanations: mass is a measure of how much matter is in an object.

140.B) constellation

Explanations: a constellation is a group of stars that form a recognizable pattern.

141.D) pulley

Explanations: a pulley is a type of simple machine that consists of a rope, cable or chain wrapped around a grooved wheel.

142.C) Earth's atmosphere

Explanations: Earth's atmosphere reflects the blue lights in the atmosphere.

143.C) tundra

Explanations: a tundra is a type of ecosystem that is typically found in very cold regions.

144.C) fern

Explanations: a fern is a type of plant that has small leaves and reproduces through spores.

145.A) Licked

Explanations: the little boy licked his ice cream cone.

146.A) Wagged

Explanations: the dog wagged his tail when he saw his owner.

147.C) Ride

Explanations: A bike can be ridden.

148.C) Carriage

Explanations: The carriage can be driven.

149.B) Arctic

Explanations: Polar bears are found in the Arctic only.

150.C) Water

Explanations: The definition of island is a soil mass surrounded by water.

Made in United States
Troutdale, OR
12/27/2023

16458716R00040